CHIEF TARIRI
The Servant Plane

by Karen Jane Lewis

Chief Tariri

Published by JAARS, Inc.
PO Box 248, Waxhaw, NC 28173

ISBN 1-55671-062-3

Cover design by Kathy McBride
Front cover photograph by June Hathersmith

First Edition April 1998

Printed in the United States of America

CHIEF TARIRI
The Servant Plane

Τhis book is dedicated to Bernie and Nancy May, and Bud and Gladys Woods.

Bernie May, long-time JAARS pilot, had the vision for using DC-3s to further the task of Bible translation and literacy. He nurtured that vision into existence. Bernie was with *Tariri* five years. He was Captain and made every flight for almost four of those years. Bernie remembers those days as one of the most fulfilling times in his ministry. Nancy May supported Bernie in all his "exploits" in Wycliffe, even when it meant a lot of time apart.

Bud and Gladys Woods, life-time JAARS mechanic, were with *Tariri* over 30 years. They were the first personnel assigned to the plane, and it has been like a member of their family ever since. Gladys even chose the colors for the plane, and JAARS liked them so much, the blues and white became the fleet colors around the world.

The Woods' quiet dedication to *Tariri*, the servant plane, came out in wry humor in a prayer letter:
"Please pray that we will know the Lord's will for us after our two-year commitment here in Kenya ends. Actually we committed to two years seven years ago, but since it ended up taking six years for us and the plane to arrive in Africa, it's hard to tell when our commitment 'ended.'"

Well, for the Woods—and the Mays—the commitment never ends. It just takes on new shape. That's because their dedication is not to an airplane or even mission aviation, but to God and the work of Bible translation and literacy.

"...those who hope in the Lord will renew their strength. They will soar on wings of eagles...." Isaiah 40:31

CONTENTS

FOREWORD:

God uses His people to carry the Gospel to the ends of the earth. To get there, God's people often use airplanes. The following story is the heartwarming account of one mission airplane, a DC-3 called *Chief Tariri*. It is the tale of the plane's crew and passengers and destinations, and the unique role it has fulfilled in the work of Christ's Kingdom.

The great missionary Paul used ships for his travels. Today aircraft such as *Chief Tariri* often are the most effective vessels for missionary travel and support.

In 1994 Samaritan's Purse was confronted by considerable logistical challenges in providing relief aid to Rwandans after that eastern African nation's brutal massacre. *Chief Tariri* helped us get the job done, and in the process, helped impart hope to those who were suffering.

JAARS—and AIM-AIR—excel at helping Christ's servants work in remote places on His behalf. *Chief Tariri* is one reason why this is true. My prayer is that this book will encourage and strengthen you as a bearer of the heavenly treasure.

—Franklin Graham

A PERSONAL FLIGHT OF FANCY

My first plane ride was on a United Airlines DC-3. I was 15 months old. In my first few years I traveled often between central California and southern Oregon on DC-3s. I've never forgotten those wonderful flights.

In 1985 the media covered the fiftieth anniversary of DC-3s. I began to see that the DC-3 is a phenomenon. It enjoys an enthusiastic "following." The plane's fascinating history captured my imagination with an unexpected grip.

I quickly learned the DC-3 is an aviation legend. Pilots adore the plane. One enthusiastic fan said, "The only substitute for an old DC-3 is another old DC-3!" One day I sat on the steps of one, on the edge of an executive-jet tarmac. Time after time, the pilots of those sleek planes walked over and wistfully asked: "May I take a look at the ol' girl?"

Then I was asked to research the DC-3. Especially *Chief Tariri,* a DC-3 owned and operated by JAARS—the technical service arm of Wycliffe Bible Translators. Tariri: I thought back to the stories I'd read of the man for whom the plane is named. Tariri: a Peruvian headhunter chief turned evangelist through the transforming power of God's Word in his mother tongue!

One of my first memories of mission aviation is of an incident that happened across the border from Chief Tariri's jungle home, in neighboring Ecuador. I clearly remember the whispered conversations of the adults in my childhood church in early 1956. They were distressed. They were talking about things that weren't meant for children's ears. But I pestered my Grandma Lewis for answers. What had happened? Why was everyone upset? What jungle were they whispering about? What men? What plane? What, what...? I kept

asking questions.

When Grandma finally told me about the death of five missionaries at the hands of the Aucas (now called Waorani) in Ecuador, my "whats" turned into "whys." Grandma didn't side-step the interrogation. She had a struggle explaining to a sensitive youngster, but somehow she managed to leave me with the feeling that God cared very much for everyone involved.

Time passed and I didn't hear much about the Aucas or South America. My church's visiting missionaries all seemed to be from Africa or Asia. My occasional, not-too-serious discussions with myself about being a missionary seemed to focus on those continents.

Then, a college pal of mine married a pilot and they joined the ranks of JAARS. I couldn't believe it. Gail was a fine musician and a good student. Why was she choosing to spend her life like that, I wondered. She and her skilled husband must be crazy! (Imagine Gail and Don Evans' surprise and pleasure when their ol' incredulous chum joined Wycliffe Bible Translators in 1981.)

Eventually I flew to the JAARS headquarters in North Carolina. I could hardly wait to see the plane named *Chief Tariri*. Soon I stood leaning on a chain-link fence, gazing at it. My deep surge of emotion astounded me. My heart seemed to expand, and yet I felt strangely shy. The plane seemed like an old friend and a superhero at the same time.

Chief Tariri! Again, I thought of the headhunter turned evangelist. And this plane named for the chief? What a rich history of service! I had the same feelings I'd felt when I first met Corrie ten Boom, and "Uncle Cam" Townsend, the founder of Wycliffe Bible Translators. I had known I was in the presence of some very special servants of the Lord. And now this servant plane almost seemed to affect me the same way. I couldn't wait to start researching and writing.

I interviewed *Chief Tariri* crew members. I wrote to dozens of other people—former crew and passengers. I searched JAARS archival material. I read everything I could about DC-3s. I visited aviation museums. I visited

Clover Field in California where the original DC-3 was born, and I hung over other fences at out-of-the-way airstrips to gaze at Threes.

In short, I fell in love with an airplane. And I rejoiced again in God's unending faithfulness to the Bibleless peoples—and to each of us! Imagine my thrill when living in Kenya several years later, I watched *Chief Tariri* touch down in Nairobi! (With friends Gail and Don, by the way.) And imagine my pleasure when it fell to me to arrange some flights for famine aid and a dedication of newly translated Scripture.

Praise God for all His blessings, including wonderful "extras" like a DC-3 named *Chief Tariri!*

THE DC-3—A LEGENDARY PLANE

1932. Planes were fabric-covered wooden structures—slow at 100 miles per hour, extremely noisy inside and subject to weather conditions. The American public was appalled when famed Notre Dame football coach Knute Rockne died in a plane crash. Emerging passenger airlines knew major changes in airplane design were needed.

Transcontinental and Western Airlines (TWA) challenged airplane designers to come up with something new. Donald Douglas jumped at the chance. After all, he and his engineer friends had built a number of planes, including the World Cruisers. The Cruisers were used by United States Army Air Service flyers in the first aerial circumnavigation of the globe in 1924.

Taking up TWA's challenge, Douglas and his group drew up a completely new design. The wing center section was built with the wing structure below the floor level, doing away with an irritating spar that ran through the cabin causing trouble for both passengers and crew. The revolutionary multi-spar wing would prove to give nearly unlimited airframe life.

TWA signed a contract with Douglas. The prototype—the Douglas Commercial—1st Model, or DC-1—had taken a mere nine months to construct. It was the biggest twin-engined land-plane built in the United States up to that time. Fortunately, reliable 700-horsepower engines had been developed. Revolutionary testing methods such as the use of a wind tunnel and the building of a full-size fuselage mock-up were utilized.

Successful test flights resulted in a TWA contract for 25 DC-2s, the improved production model of the DC-1. The DC-2 cut the 44-hour travel time between

1

southern California and New York to less than 18 hours.

The plane was far more comfortable than any before. Cabin noise levels were good. Vents allowed the interior air to be changed every minute. Seating was comfortable, and each passenger had a window. In the rear of the plane was a toilet and basin room.

As airlines vied for customers, they constantly called for planes with greater passenger capacity and comfort, plus more speed and range. It was not long before American Airlines introduced Pullman-like sleeper berths.

In 1934, American Airlines president C.R. Smith was aware of the public's demand for more aircraft comfort and capacity. In a long phone call ($335.50's worth—a lot of money then), Smith persuaded Douglas to expand the DC-2. By 1935 Douglas and his engineers had "stretched" and widened the DC-2, converting it to a DC-3. Only 10 percent of its parts were compatible with the DC-2. The DC-3 took its first flight on December 17, 1935, the thirty-second anniversary of the Wright brothers' historic flight.

The DC-3 was bigger, stronger and more powerful than the DC-2. The National Air and Space Museum in Washington, D.C. likes to say the DC-3 weighs more than two adult elephants and cruises at 180 miles per hour. The Boeing 747 weighs as much as 90 elephants and flies at 600 miles per hour.

As for hours of flying time: one DC-3 delivered in 1937 has logged over 90,000 flying hours. It's thought to be the world's highest-time transport.

The DC-3 enjoyed immediate popularity. On June 25, 1936, American Airlines got in ahead of TWA and placed the first large order. One week later, Donald Douglas received aviation's *Collier Trophy* in the office of President Franklin D. Roosevelt for developing "the most outstanding twin-engined transport plane."

Orders poured in to Douglas from all the major airlines. By 1938 the DC-3 dominated the United States domestic market. The planes provided 95 percent of all scheduled services. A year later DC-3s were used by 30 overseas airlines, accounting for 90 percent of the

world's airline traffic. The DC-3 would go into the history books as the grandfather of modern passenger aviation. It has been said the DC-3 taught the public to fly.

As war threatened in 1939, Douglas also received orders for variations of the plane. By the time Pearl Harbor was attacked in 1941, the company had built 266 DC-3s and 164 C-47 and R-4D variants of the DC-3. Previous contracts for nearly 150 more planes for commercial use were taken over by the military. Many DC-3s already in airline service also were "recruited" for the war effort.

The first contract for the DC-3 variant C-47 came at the height of the Battle of Britain. A year later another 1,900 planes were ordered. Douglas plants in Santa Monica and Long Beach, California, and Oklahoma City, Oklahoma, eventually built an incredible total of over 10,000 DC-3s and C-47 variants between 1935 and 1947.

The DC-3 had been nicknamed "Dizzy Three" by airline pilots and called "Placid Plodder," "Old

Methuselah," and "Dowager Duchess" by others. During World War II, American GIs affectionately named the DC-3 "Gooney Bird" and Commonwealth troops called them "Dakotas."

The DC-3 was cherished by both pilots and passengers alike. Any pilot who has ever flown a DC-3 is "in love" with her the rest of his life. Forgiving of just about any kind of mistreatment, the DC-3 is stable with a capital "S". One of the most comforting characteristics of the DC-3 is its ability to fly on one engine. Military records also reveal scores of wartime stories of C-47s flying full of holes, without wing tips, with control cables broken—and once, with one DC-3 wing and one DC-2 wing!

During World War II, DC-3s were called on to tow gliders, drop paratroopers, fly out the wounded, and drop supplies. The full scope of wartime cargo is impossible to list. Incalculable tonnage of standard supplies was flown. And the list of unusual cargo is amazing: sometimes entertaining and often touching. Live mules were parachuted into Burma. Sixteen

hundred pounds of sheep were hauled for Christmas dinner in a jungle. And lipsticks were dropped to medics to mark instructions on wounded troops' foreheads.

Log books show DC-3s serving around the globe during the war. They were involved in the Allied landings in North Africa, the invasion of Sicily, and flew behind the Japanese lines in Burma. The plane also flew the "Hump" supply line crossing the Himalayas between India and China.

Pan American Airlines DC-3 crews ferried time-expired or flight-exhausted military pilots back to bases. One Royal Air Force pilot recalled taking a DC-3 ferry flight from Egypt to Sudan, across Chad and into Nigeria, then to Sierra Leone and Liberia to catch a ship convoy going north!

On D-Day—June 6, 1944—1,200 DC-3 variants rose into the air, four abreast in a 200-mile column. Twenty-thousand troops were on board. The exploits of the DC-3 during World War II are legendary. General Dwight D. Eisenhower said the plane was one of the 10 reasons the Allies won the war!

As soon as the war ended, DC-3s began carrying Allied prisoners of war out of former combat zones. Airfields in England, for instance, which had been sending bombers into Europe, now received men for medical care.

As the post-war activities wound down, airlines were eager to get back their DC-3s. However, they soon found newer planes, and relegated the DC-3s to second and third-line service. But the "living legend" was not to be kept down. DC-3s flew during the Berlin Airlift in 1948-49 and right through the Korean war. Even during the Vietnam conflict they flew as gunships in the heat of the battle.

Today an estimated 1,500 DC-3s are flying, or are flyable, in over 40 nations. Many countries use the "old faithfuls" for passenger air service. Hundreds are carrying cargo across frozen terrain and steamy jungles, scorching deserts and tropical beaches. They continue to fly through appalling conditions and land on every tough surface imaginable. Some DC-3s are used for

aerial photography and survey. Others do crop dusting, fight forest fires or spray dispersant on oil spills on the oceans.

Meanwhile, "nostalgia" flights are offered to DC-3 fans in many places. And magazine advertisements seeking "the good old days look" frequently use a DC-3 as a backdrop for their product.

Film and television producers continue to find excuses to include DC-3s in their plans. *Police Academy 5,* for instance, used a DC-3 to fly pigs, goats, chickens and 22 toilet seats to the Bahamas. Similar to some of the DC-3s' wartime assignments, really.

There is no doubt the DC-3 is an aviation legend. Truly it is, as someone has said, "the plane that changed the world."

JAARS IS BORN

A small boy leaned on the airfield fence and watched the "flying machines." Young Cameron Townsend dreamed of soaring with the birds himself one day.

Years later, in the mid-1920s, aviation remained a novelty. While fascinated with airplanes, most people were not rushing to trust their lives to the "rubber band jobs." But Cameron Townsend was different. As early as 1926, he was eager to use airplanes in his fledgling mission efforts. By 1930 Townsend was planning an "Airplane Crusade to the Unevangelized Jungle-Lands of Latin America." Fellow mission and church leaders had varied reactions. One administrator of a Central American mission wrote to Townsend:

> "Regarding the possibility of airplane transportation for reaching the out-of-the-way missionary

districts, it is possible that the future may hold something for us along that line. However, at the present writing I must confess that I had rather go overland, even if I had to walk. I haven't been anxious to go up in a plane. Mr. B made the suggestion that he would like to get a plane for traveling over Honduras. When Miss G told us about it, she referred to it as a sure sign of Mr. B's backsliding, explaining that she had known Mr. B to be one of the best evangelizers she had ever traveled along the country road with, that he never missed an opportunity to give out a tract and

personal word of testimony as he passed travelers and homes along the roadside. She felt that his going by airplane would hinder the ministry."

Someone else wrote:

"Your missionary friend (Townsend) has the right spirit and his idea to use a plane is sound...There is no doubt in my mind that the airplane will be one of the greatest assets to missionaries in their work and particularly in Central and South America where terrestrial transportation is so difficult and conditions so primitive. I highly endorse its use in (this)...case."

Townsend found a man willing to learn to fly for the crusade. He wrote enthusiastically:

"Mr. R. Lynn Van Sickle, a graduate of Moody Bible Institute and a member of their radio staff, is taking flying lessons in preparation to take part in the Crusade. He got in touch with a consecrated Christian aviator who has been in South America and believes in our project and who promised to teach him to fly for the cost of gasoline, etc. They flew up into northern Wisconsin and camped out, concentrating on the lessons for two weeks so that by now Van Sickle must be pretty good at the controls. He is an auto mechanic already so he should learn rapidly."

Townsend's attitudes toward learning to fly might seem rather naive or cavalier, but they merely reflected the times. People either were frightened by the idea of flying or felt it was "simple as can be." Too, Townsend firmly believed that if God calls you to a task, He goes ahead of you in it.

13

The aviation evangelistic crusade was a success. Sixteen years later, Townsend had established Wycliffe Bible Translators and already had personnel in Mexico and Peru. In July 1946 he was generating support for an amphibian airplane in Peru:

> "...With this powerful airplane, our base in the jungle will be within an hour and a half of Lima. A two-day hard trip over the 15,000-foot hump where mountain sickness is common is converted into a pleasant outing and the cost is reduced to one-fourth of the automobile fare. The allocating of the workers among the different tribes along the inland rivers will be done in one-fiftieth of the time it would take by the ordinary means of travel. Praise God for the amphibian and for the Christian Airmen's Missionary Fellowship.

> These consecrated ex-service pilots are amputating the "im" from the dreaded word so often applied to jungle missionary work in the past—IMPOSSIBLE."

In 1947 Townsend and his wife Elaine and their infant daughter Grace were involved in a commercial airplane accident in Mexico. Townsend and Elaine suffered multiple fractures. Fortunately, little Grace was unharmed. Still in the rubble of the plane, Townsend called out to a colleague, "Quick! Get a camera. People need to know we need our own planes."

Soon Townsend wrote home:

> "The first thing after the accident, while lying on the ground waiting to be carried to this hut, I thought: 'God is going to use this accident to arouse greater interest in providing adequate aviation for our young pioneers.'

> "As never before we must

expect for their transportation the best pilots and the best equipment...We are absolutely dependent on aviation for our great pioneering projects in inaccessible areas, but I don't see how we can afford to have such accidents as this. May God enable us to do our best and then trust Him to do the rest."

Later Townsend wrote:

"No one thinks of going to the North Pole any more in dog sleds and we have passed the dog sled stage of missionary endeavor. It was too expensive and too hopeless. Too many lives were lost also. To advance with airplanes and radio communication is the safest and most economical way in the Amazonian jungle."

It wasn't long before the Bible translation and literacy task had the vital support of aviation. Thus it was that in 1948 JAARS (Jungle Aviation and Radio Service) was born.

In 1964 JAARS pilot Bernie May added his own dream to the picture. He could see that a larger plane than JAARS was currently using could save missionaries money, time and energy. He believed DC-3 airplanes were prime candidates for mission service. The DC-3 always had been able to do more for what it cost than any other plane. A strong landing gear and an ability to land on short, rough runways gave the plane tremendous versatility. And it could carry heavy loads of cargo—about one-third of its weight.

In 1964, after God had performed a series of financial miracles, a DC-3 was bought by JAARS. The plane's registration number was changed to N2000L. The 2000 was intended to reflect the then-estimated 2,000 language groups still without God's Word.

After a special dedication of the plane in February 1965 at the Philadelphia International Airport, Bernie

May climbed into the cockpit. When Ground Control called on the radio and asked about the ceremony, May told them where the plane was headed and what it would be doing. Another pilot ready to taxi called on the radio: "Two Thousand Lima, this is United right behind you in the lineup. We want to say our prayers go with you, sir." Pilot after pilot came on the air, wishing the DC-3 and its crew their best. Finally, as the plane was about to take off, the tower added: "DC-3 Two Thousand Lima, cleared for takeoff—and may the Lord bless you, sir."

What a great start of the plane's new career. DC-3s once were used in warfare. Now one would fly to offer God's peace. It would be called *Tariri*.

TARIRI, THE SERVANT CHIEF

A strange roaring sound filled the air above the Peruvian jungle. Indians stood transfixed as two objects—half-bird, half-canoe—swept across the sky. Bravely stepping out, Chief Tariri led his people down to the river to see the float planes land.

Tariri later recalled: "As we came along in our canoes...our eyes nearly popped out! We had never seen such things like that before. They shone white in the sunlight, two of them.

"We saw people in the two 'canoes.' It is probably a chief, we thought. Only a chief would have a 'canoe' like that. We looked and looked.

"The people climbed up the bank and stood there. As we looked, there stood Monchanki and Mpawachi (Wycliffe Bible translators Lorrie Anderson and Doris Cox). 'Who are they?', we thought, and we stared. We never had seen such dresses. Their dresses were long

and they looked like *shoroshoro* birds that swish their tails as they walk to and fro.

"They grabbed our hands. Why do they do that? They might put us in the canoes. Worried like a child, I let my hand fall. I was thinking many things. There was once a man who came and took people to work for him. Maybe these had the same thing in mind.

"We thought of running away. We talked among ourselves. I asked Victorino (the contact man), 'What is this all about? Tell us.'

"'They came to tell you good news,' he said, 'but you will have to teach them your language. When they have learned Shapra, then they will tell you. It is about God. All of you listen.'"

Chief Tariri normally wasn't afraid of other people. In fact, he was one of the most brave and powerful men in his tribe. Usually it was Chief Tariri making shrill

sounds in the jungle, not airplanes. Chief Tariri was a killer, a headhunter.

At 10 years old, Tariri was told: "If people come to your house to attack, do not be afraid. You just chase them back into the woods and kill them. If you do not kill them, they will kill you."

From that time, Tariri went on killing raids. He personally avenged the murder of his two brothers. He attained—and maintained—his position as chief by killing enemies. One day he told Lorrie how he and other Shapras took the heads of their enemies, removed the skulls, and shrank them to the size of a doubled-up fist. Those heads became valued war trophies. He said it was good to hang a shrunken head in your house and drink and dance around it.

As leader of his family, Chief Tariri was expected to work "white magic" to bring healing and to control the elements and jungle creatures. Sometimes the people got well. Sometimes they did not.

Many days Chief Tariri's chants to the spirit of the anaconda water boa pierced the jungle:

"You dweller in darkness
You have taken this child's spirit,
His spirit you have stolen to hide
 down deep
In the watery darkness where you
 dwell.
But now I defy you!
I now bring back the spirit of the
 sick one!"

Thus it was that Chief Tariri existed in a cycle of both taking lives and trying to save others. Against this background, Tariri learned to appreciate Lorrie and Doris and what they were trying to do. He gave a lot of time to the two women. Little by little, Lorrie and Doris built up their understanding of the language. They told Chief Tariri about God's Son. They told him about Jesus calming the wind and sea. They told him about Jesus healing the blind and lame. They told him about Lazarus being raised from the dead. "What kind of person was this Jesus?" Chief Tariri pondered.

One day Lorrie was attacked by an anaconda, a

deadly water boa. She sustained scores of tiny puncture wounds as it struck again and again. Finally, the snake gripped her and was about to squeeze her to death. Then the miraculous happened: the anaconda—never known to release a victim—did just that!

Later, as Lorrie was being treated, there was a commotion outside the door. A woman from another village pushed her way into the house to see Lorrie. "We didn't learn what that was all about until some time later," Lorrie recalls. "It seems her husband, a witch doctor from a different language group, was angry with us. On that morning he had chanted to the spirit of the anaconda and sent the giant snake to kill me. I'm certain that, except for the power of God, it would have worked."

Chief Tariri agreed with Lorrie. Remembering his own days of calling on the snake's spirit, he said: "The spirit of the anaconda is very great and very powerful, but God is greater."

Another day Chief Tariri heard the story of the crucifixion. Later he repeated the story to his friends.

"When they wanted to kill Jesus, they did just what we used to do," he said. The Shapras always called a big meeting to plan killings. Referring to the spearing of Jesus' side, Tariri said: "You see, way back in those days they used the same kind of spears we use now!" The Good News was making sense to him. It was completely relevant to his life.

Chief Tariri was delighted when Lorrie and Doris made their first attempts at Bible translation and tested it out with him. "When you tell me God's Word, I am happy," he said.

Chief Tariri's heart was moved when he heard the Scriptures in his own language, but still he hesitated about giving his life to Jesus. He already had been threatened by other warriors for giving up the old ways. Still, Chief Tariri kept saying things like, "When we accept God's Word, we will leave drinking completely." Doris often wondered what was holding him back from a commitment.

A year later Chief Tariri returned from hunting and found Doris waiting for him. Months before, when he

had listened to the very first verse of Scripture translated into Shapra, he had said: "When you talk like that, my heart leaps with understanding."

Now Doris pleaded, "Brother, please come here quickly." Chief Tariri, still covered in mud and monkey blood from his hunting, wondered what could be so urgent. He sat down across from Doris. "Can you tell me how to say 'Do you want to receive Jesus into your heart?'" she asked.

Chief Tariri gave her the sentence. She wrote it down and read it back for approval. But Chief Tariri didn't tell her it was correct. Instead, he looked at her and said, "Yes, I want very much to receive Jesus into my heart."

And so the powerful warrior became a humble child of God. Later Chief Tariri said, "Why should even a chief say, 'I am a chief?' How can a person be greater than God? We cannot live without Him."

Chief Tariri became a servant leader, teaching and evangelizing his own people. He told them: "We were afraid to die. We talked about it with fear. Who is there that is not afraid to die? A chief is not supposed to be afraid to die. But when it comes right down to it, chiefs are afraid to die. Now, if you die, you go to be with God. That is what we believe."

Tariri taught his children to trust in God, not witch doctors. "I cannot chant any more," he said. "Now we think of medicine and we talk to God. He helps the children get better. I remind them that God is great and that He Himself wants to make them well."

Talking about the old beliefs, Chief Tariri commented: "The ancestors told us many things about the boa, the toucan, the jaguar, the possum, the ocelot and the earthquake. We thought these gave long life. I do not tell my children those things. I tell them to talk to God, to talk in Jesus' name. God gives you the kind of life by which you will never die."

"The thing to teach is God's Word," he continued. "The thing to tell is about the life that God gives us, the life by which He takes care of us. When your heart is not right before God, you are living bad. Talk to God. He straightens people out, even the very bad kind. It is

possible for one's bad heart to be cleansed by the blood of Jesus. God's Word tells us what to do. God's Word also tells us what not to do."

Thinking about his ancestors, he asked Doris: "Why did you people not come long ago? If you had told us long ago, the old ones would have known it, too."

Chief Tariri's evangelistic witness became a missionary zeal as he reached out to neighboring groups. He constantly thanked God for sending missionaries to give his people the Scriptures. He prayed that others would be called into Bible translation work. "If all the chiefs would start sending people out with God's Word, then Jesus would be happy and return."

It's no wonder the JAARS DC-3 was named *Tariri*. A "chief" among airplanes took the name of an Indian chief dramatically transformed by the power of God's Word. Both would take God's Word to Bibleless people.

TARIRI, THE SERVANT PLANE

Tariri was a servant plane from its first day with the Bible translation and literacy team. Based in Miami, Florida, for a year and a half, the plane made regular flights between the United States and South American countries, as well as flights within some of those countries.

In 1966 *Tariri* moved to Ecuador to support the Bible translation and literacy efforts from there. Don Johnson, former director of the work in Ecuador, recalls: "When we were thinking about the possibility of having *Tariri* come, we kind of gazed at the ceiling and wondered if we could use the plane two or three times a year. But, wow, during peak periods, the plane made two or three flights a day. I'm a great champion of the DC-3. It changed our ministry in Ecuador! The flexibility it gave us was marvelous."

John Lindskoog, director of the Ecuador work when *Tariri* arrived, also recalls the difference the plane made to the translation effort: "The availability of that dear old Gooney Bird revolutionized life for us. It cut flight time across the Andes. We could transport people and materials safely and effectively. We could serve everyone better. Why, the plane was even involved in some search and rescue operations!"

Continuing, Lindskoog says: "I still remember the thrill of using *Tariri* to locate some of the downriver Waorani (formerly known as Auca). Though this segment lived separately from the rest, they were part of the same language group involved in the deaths of the five missionaries in '56. Later, believers from the first group of Waorani went to their 'cousins' with the Good News in their own language.

"Another way *Tariri* served faithfully," adds Linkskoog, "was in the Ecuadorian government's

bilingual education program. We cooperated with the education officials in training teachers from every language group. Each summer the DC-3 served by carrying teacher trainees to their schooling at our jungle center, Limoncocha. Government officials could leave Quito on *Tariri* in the morning, visit the training program and be back in their offices by late afternoon. It was of invaluable service to them and built up many good relationships."

Don Johnson also remembers the pleasure of serving Ecuador by helping facilitate that bilingual education training, as well as medical and dental care, and courses in carpentry, mechanics and first aid. He recalls: "Once an Ecuadorian senator told me after a visit via the DC-3, 'I used to oppose your work, but now that I've seen you and know what you're doing, I want you to know you have a friend in my office.'"

Johnson also says: "I have wonderful memories of seeing the language group trainees and their families out by the DC-3 getting ready to return to their home areas. Each family was there with woven baskets of fish they had caught in the lake and dried, and also butchered wild pigs...precious commodities since protein sources were scarce in their areas. They also had their school supplies, wooden suitcases they had made in the carpentry course, and even volleyballs. There was a lot of excited noise! Of course they had made a lot of new friends from the other language groups."

Ask any of the missionaries who served in Ecuador about *Tariri* and their faces light up. Everyone has a favorite story. Some are just plain fun. Some are dramatic and many include medical emergencies and evacuations. A lot of the memories are touching for a mixture of reasons.

There were the "Ark Flights," for instance. Bovines and Bibles? Yes, more than once, *Tariri* became a flying Noah's Ark to support mission work. Herb Brussow, a Wycliffe missionary, served as an Intercultural Community Development Specialist in South America. He helped train local people in new farming techniques. Brussow had the DC-3 transport animals, male and female.

Tariri also transported the Brussows' tools and family goods to a farm in Colombia. "Bonaire Farm was named after a Trans-World Radio transmitting station in the Caribbean," Brussow explains. "It couldn't have been more appropriate. The farm was developed to offer practical helps for the Indian people where our translators were serving. Most of all we wanted the farm to be like the TWR station: transmitting the Gospel message of Christian concern to the Indians and all of Colombia."

For nearly 30 years, Bonaire Farm acted as a catalyst between isolated Indian groups and various Colombian agencies. Indian leaders have been prepared to help their own people. Those groups, cut off from most of the world by their location and language, desperately need practical help in the areas of food production, health care and literacy.

Bonaire Farm took root in the Colombian soil. Its ministry has brought forth "fruit" across the country. National literature is full of references to the desire of the people to have their own land and animals and crops. That desire has been met by scores of people at Bonaire. But, in addition, lives have been changed by the transforming power of Christ. One young man returned to his home and reported that Christianity was not just a foreigner's religion. He told his family that he had met Indians from other areas and Spanish-speaking Colombians who were Christians. Later, he accepted Christ as his Savior.

Pilot Bernie May recalls: "Those 'Ark Flights' were really fun. They were about as noisy as it can get. I had a new empathy with Noah. Noah was bouncing around out there on the water, and we were bouncing around in the sky with these animals. Yes, I had a real empathy for Noah. And we couldn't fly with the windows open!

"But you know," Bernie continues, "Bottom line, it was a blessing to know we were helping give the Indians a new beginning—a beginning of a whole new world; a better, healthier life in more ways than one."

Another time, the DC-3 crew was less than thrilled with its animal passengers. They were asked to

exchange a dozen bulls between two mission farms in Ecuador. One farm was on the coast and the other was over the Andes in the jungle. The two herds were becoming too inbred. Thus the transfer.

At the time, Bernie May remembered a report of a cattle flight made by another mission. The plane had nearly crashed when the livestock broke loose in the cabin. The bulls had stampeded forward and back, finally breaking through the rear door and falling to their deaths.

Bernie did not want that to happen to *Tariri,* or the animals. He told the missionary farmers: "We'll fly the bulls on three conditions. One, they're tranquilized. Two, they're completely tied down in the plane. And three, you'll sit with them with a gun trained on them. One of them starts to get loose, and you shoot him! No questions asked."

Everyone agreed to the plan. Then, just before the flight, Bernie was asked to make a medical emergency flight on a different plane. Fellow pilot Virg Gottfried took the bull exchange flight.

No sooner had the plane lifted into the air, than the farmer became violently airsick. Laughing all these years later, Bernie says: "Then the bulls got sick. At both ends. You've never seen a greener farmer, when that plane landed. Or a greener bull, for that matter. It took us a week to get the plane smelling normal and not like a barnyard. To this day, Virg thinks I knew what would happen and set him up!"

Not all of *Tariri's* flights included a humor factor. Many were a matter of life and death. One day a radio message came into Quito: JAARS pilot Paul Duffey had crashed at the jungle center. He had been practicing a "dead stick" landing when a down draft caught him. He had severe back injuries.

The DC-3 was sent to bring Paul into Quito and then he was evacuated to the United States. He received excellent medical care, but was never able to walk again.

Two years after the accident, Paul sat in his wheelchair wearing a NASA hard hat. Almost holding his breath, he anxiously watched a bright yellow

twin-engine airplane. It hung suspended 160 feet above a concrete apron at NASA's Langley Research Center in Hampton, Virginia.

"I knew what was going to happen," Paul says, "but I had to brace myself. I'll never forget it. The experimental crash was awful—right in front of us. We saw it all: the pieces flying, the dummy occupants thrashing about, the whole bit. My stomach was tied in knots."

The NASA test crash brought back the painful memories of his own dead-stick accident in the Ecuador jungle. But this crash was a carefully engineered plan. NASA was testing a seat specially-designed by JAARS and Mission Aviation Fellowship (MAF) to provide protection against lower spine injuries like Paul's.

"We thank the Lord for the opportunity to reach into the unknown with NASA to make flying safer," Paul says. "If my accident brought all this into focus for JAARS—if all I've been through contributes to this—it's been worth it."

Sheri Borman Larsen, a Wycliffe "missionary kid" who grew up in Ecuador, remembers *Tariri* roaring into the air to pick up Paul at the jungle center. She says: "I heard the DC-3 leave at an unusually late time of day and realized there must be an emergency somewhere. We all started praying, even though we didn't know what to pray about." The DC-3 only had a small part in Paul's story, but it was typical of the plane to be ready to serve in any situation.

Sheri also remembers a fun *Tariri* flight: "A bunch of the missionary kids who were at a boarding school in Quito flew out to the jungle center on the DC-3 for the Christmas vacation. As *Tariri* taxied in, the pilot put on a Santa Claus mask. When the plane stopped, he leaned out of the window and yelled 'Merry Christmas' to all the parents gathered there at the airstrip. I guess he knew he was delivering the 'presents' they wanted most for Christmas—the kids who had been away for months!"

Another holiday, the *Tariri* pilots really went the extra mile, or 300 miles in this case. When they flew

the MKs back to Quito, there was an epidemic in the city and schools were closed for a week. What did the pilots do? They turned right around and took the youngsters back to the jungle center for a bonus week with their parents!

Sheri's parents, Bub and Bobbie Borman, were translating the Scriptures for the Cofan people. One day word came to the administrative offices in Limoncocha and Quito that Emma Chica, a Cofan teenager, had been bitten by a highly poisonous "bushmaster" snake. Missionary doctors managed to save her life but not the wounded leg. Eventually Emma was fitted with a locally-made peg leg and flown to Limoncocha. There she learned to use her new leg. And she learned to read. Emma learned something else. She began to understand about God's love. "Mrs. Borman talked to me in my own language about Christ," Emma recalls. "I had heard about Christ at the hospital, but did not really understand because it was not in my language."

Soon Emma gave her heart to God. She said she had learned to trust Him by watching His love in the lives of her missionary friends. She immediately felt a desire to tell others about Christ.

When Emma returned to the Cofan area, she began to witness to her relatives and friends about her newfound faith. Many people could see the changes in Emma's life. But others made fun of her and gave her a hard time. She struggled to maintain her faith and not give in to the "fun" of unbelievers.

Time passed and the jungle humidity took its toll on Emma's wood and leather artificial leg. People with artificial limbs were rare in the jungle so more weather-resistant pieces were not available in the country. When Wycliffe Associates (a lay organization which aids Wycliffe Bible Translators) heard about Emma's need, they raised money for a flight on *Tariri* to Florida and made arrangements for Emma's medical care and housing.

Emma was pleased not only about her new artificial leg, but also about the opportunity to be around Christians. "I was happy while I was in Florida. I was away from those that talked bad about me. And I was

asked to speak in churches. It was hard. But I also thought I needed to go back and talk to my mother's family and tell them more about Christ. So when I returned, every evening I faithfully gathered the folks to talk about Christ. I gave up the things that were not what God wanted me to do and became happy."

At one point, Emma expressed her gratefulness for the help and influence of her missionary friends in a poem:

> "O Limoncocha, the beautiful lake
> of the Oriente;
> O *Tariri,* precious in my Ecuador,
> I hope that you will shine as a star
> In the villages of Ecuador."

Roy Minor piloted *Tariri* the day Emma returned to Limoncocha after she came back from the States. "It felt good," he recalled, "to be involved in helping Emma. I didn't hear much about her, but I thought about her often afterwards. However, I didn't think of her when I received a call at my office at the JAARS center in North Carolina years later."

"Roy," the operator said, "I thought you'd be interested: There seems to be an 'evangelist' among the Cofan, really witnessing to people."

Roy's response was a bit skeptical. "I don't see how that can be," he said. "There's little interest in Christianity among the Cofan. And there's certainly no Cofan evangelist. Thanks for calling, but I think you have the wrong language group."

Somewhat bemused, the radio operator decided to get a confirmation of the first message. Again, the answer came back from Ecuador: "Yes, there is evangelism going on."

Still unable to believe it, Roy went to the radio room and called Ecuador himself. "Yes," they said, "God is using Emma Chica to witness to her own people!"

It was not unusual for *Tariri* to play a small, but vital part in a much larger story like Emma's. The crew members were oriented to serving in whatever way they could. Bernie May says: "I have always considered myself a 'Bible translator.' That affects you

in your work, in your willingness to prioritize your time and life. Every pilot wants to fly, to transport people and cargo, and so forth. But we realized we were there to serve Bible translation and literacy, not just to fly a plane."

Continuing, Bernie says: "Basically, that perspective helps you see opportunities to serve the cause of Bible translation, not the task of flying. That viewpoint helps you prioritize your time and feel good about what you're doing. The critical question for me always has been, not am I doing what I want to do, but rather am I doing what needs to be done?"

Bernie's attitude has been reflected by all *Tariri* crew members. It is a major reason why the plane has such a tremendous track record of service.

Eventually, the day came when Wycliffe missionaries were finishing up their work in Ecuador. What would happen to faithful *Tariri?*

JAARS administrators had been studying the mission transportation situation in eastern Africa. "Maybe *Tariri* could be of service there," they thought.

Former JAARS director, Martin Huyett, recalls the survey he made in cooperation with Africa Inland Mission's aviation program AIM-AIR: "The vast distances impressed me. Enormous distances! The roads in many places are just tracks, almost impassable. A journey that takes minutes or hours in a plane can take days or weeks—even months—in a four-wheel drive vehicle!"

Continuing, Huyett says: "The need for linguistics and translation and literacy in the local languages is tremendous. I came away convinced work in the local languages is essential for the future of Africa. And air transportation is essential to move ahead."

JAARS was pleased to receive AIM-AIR's invitation to join forces to meet the need. Plans began to send the *Tariri.* Personnel in Kenya asked if the name could be slightly altered. They wondered if the word "Chief" could be added? The addition would be appreciated by African people who greatly respect their chiefs. So *Chief Tariri* was scheduled to take up a new ministry in eastern Africa.

Chief Tariri and Lorrie Anderson at translation desk

Commercial plane crash in 1947, in southern Mexico

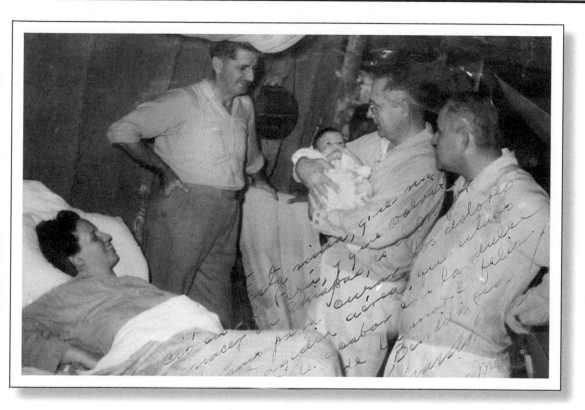

Elaine Townsend and baby Grace receive visitors after the plane crash

Dedication of *Tariri*, Bernie May speaking

Ecuador's Minister of Education arriving for a teacher training graduation

Bobbie Borman and Cofan women

Pilot Roy Minor delivers the Cofan Gospel of John to translator Bub Borman

Mechanic
Jim Miller
checks over *Tariri*

Tariri, medical trip in Ecuador

Chief Tariri, crashed in the cornfield

Chief Tariri,
rededication for
African service

Chief Tariri's first landing in Kenya

Transporting
missionaries and
children in
eastern Africa

Bud Woods, with Rendille warriors in Kenya

Chief Tariri, with
Franklin Graham (l.)
and Samaritan's
Purse team—
Rwanda

Franklin Graham
with Rwandan
children

RED CROSS ONE

Hurricane Hugo gave the JAARS headquarters in North Carolina a wallop in 1989. But the damage was nothing compared to that suffered by the people of the Caribbean islands. Eighteen hours of winds, reaching at times in excess of 200 miles per hour, left unbelievable devastation. Over 47,000 houses were destroyed or damaged, and nearly a thousand people were hospitalized. Vital services were wiped out.

Churches in the United States began to contact JAARS to charter *Chief Tariri,* which was "home" preparing for the new assignment in eastern Africa. How could JAARS say "no"? On September 27 *Chief Tariri* left Fort Lauderdale, Florida, in the predawn darkness. At twilight the crew eased the plane onto a tiny airstrip between cliff walls and the ocean on Montserrat.

"I've had nothing to feed my baby for three days," a young mother sobbed as she gratefully received canned formula. The crew thanked the Lord for another opportunity to serve.

As the first days after the hurricane passed, *Chief Tariri* was used constantly. Then the Red Cross approached the crew: would they stay on longer? With power and phone lines down, roads blocked and aircraft destroyed, linking Red Cross centers was almost impossible. Too, family members outside the hurricane area were not able to contact their loved ones. The DC-3 could be used to carry messages.

JAARS responded to the Red Cross wholeheartedly. Twice-daily round trips from San Juan, Puerto Rico to the other islands began. *Chief Tariri* carried personnel, food, medical supplies, generators, portable toilets, tarps, cots, lanterns, water, blankets, clothing, mail and

much more. Most of all, it carried friendship and hope.

Soon *Chief Tariri* became known as "Red Cross One." One worker said, "They were our lifeline, our only connection with the outside world." Several of the plane's crew had served in South America and could speak Spanish, a bonus in the relief efforts.

During the weeks in the Caribbean, *Chief Tariri* made 208 trips, carrying 1,152 passengers and 153,163 pounds of cargo. When the plane and crew returned to North Carolina, the director of the Red Cross Caribbean relief operation enthused: "Throughout my life I will have many memories of this, the largest (thus far) Red Cross relief effort, and the one thing that truly tied this job together—the DC-3."

Pilot Jim Rainsberger said, "We were in the right place at the right time. The DC-3 was the airplane the Red Cross needed, capable of carrying either passengers or cargo, or both. It opened the way for us to show the love of Christ. We felt we were doing what Jesus did—helping people with their immediate needs. We will never be the same again. We must serve one another."

CRASH LANDING IN A CORNFIELD

*C*hief Tariri was about to leave for eastern Africa. The plane had been on its way a long time, but one thing after another had delayed its departure. Finally, during the summer of 1991, everything pointed to readiness. Little did anyone know, one more challenge would have to be faced.

In August *Chief Tariri* flew to a "Missions at the Airport" event near Kidron, Ohio. Rides on the DC-3 always were popular at these events. This time the JAARS team was especially eager to fly a number of "friends" of the plane who lived in the area. These men, women, boys and girls had supported the DC-3 program with their prayers and gifts for a long time. Now they would be able to have a short flight before the plane left for Africa.

Lines of eager passengers grew longer rather than shorter as the day went by. *Chief Tariri* was loaded with 24 passengers as it thundered into another take-off. Carole Rainsberger, wife of one of the pilots, watched from the ground. Then, as the plane was half way down the runway, Carole sensed something was wrong.

Just as the plane rose from the ground, it veered to the left toward some tall trees. The left engine had failed at the most critical time possible. The good engine, still under full power, was pulling the plane to the left. Pilots Don Evans and Jim Rainsberger were doing everything they could to gain some altitude. Carole—and probably a lot of other people on the ground—was praying: "Help them, Lord. Help them clear those trees."

Don Evans says, "The Lord did help us. I believe the Lord put His hand under us and lifted us over. We clipped the tops of those trees but we made it."

The plane was over the trees, but Don had to make a split-second decision. "All I could see was a wall of green," he recalls. "With the climb and mowing the tops out of those trees, we lost so much airspeed I knew there was no way we could continue single-engine. We had to put *Chief Tariri* down."

When Carole saw the plane disappear behind the trees, she fully expected to see it climb into sight again. But it didn't. She continued to pray, "Dear Lord, keep them safe."

Suddenly she saw a white cloud roll up beyond the trees. Had there been a fire or explosion?

No, no fire or explosion! The white cloud was dust stirred up as the plane slid sideways to a stop. Don had landed the plane in a cornfield, planted by an Amish farmer!

"That corn," explains Don, "was six to eight feet tall and made an excellent arresting gear. We slid in there like a big corn knife and mowed down nearly half an acre, but it stopped us—quick. In 145 feet, they told me later. It was the shortest flight I ever made. In just 47 seconds we turned a beautiful DC-3 into an expensive corn harvester. But praise the Lord for that corn. Just beyond it stood another row of trees. Trying to cut them down would have been another story."

All 24 passengers and the three crew members stepped off the plane unharmed. The plane itself was damaged. Props were bent and an engine torn loose. The landing gear also was bent and ripped. There was some structural damage.

Experts assured Don he had done everything exactly right in the split-seconds he had. "I'm glad for that," Don says. "I'm glad everyone got out okay. It could have been a terrible tragedy, but God had other plans. Everyone was telling me what a good job I did. Of course I appreciated that, but in spite of their expressions of support, I felt terrible. The last thing a pilot wants to do is bend his bird, and I'd bent this one pretty bad. It sure hurt."

Don wasn't alone in his hurt. Most people involved in the *Chief Tariri* program, directly or indirectly, had moments of wondering what in the world was going

on. Praise for God's faithfulness during the accident often was accompanied by thoughts about Satan's attacks. Too, people wondered if they had misunderstood God's will. There had been so many delays and problems. "Was the plane really not meant to go to eastern Africa?" they asked themselves.

News of the crash flashed around the Wycliffe world. Rumors started: "The plane is beyond repair," and, "The plane will be sold for scrap." People in Kenya wept when they heard the rumors.

JAARS administrators quickly moved to squelch the stories. They sent out the message: "We see this accident as opposition from the 'great opposer' and view it only as an 'interruption.'"

On that hot summer day when the white cloud rolled up beyond the trees, nine-year-old Travis Haynie went cold with fear. Only that morning he had joyfully flown from North Carolina to Ohio. He and his JAARS-assigned dad Wayne had grown to love *Chief Tariri* as they watched it over the years. One day Travis and his dad had walked around the plane in the hangar. Then,

reaching around one of the tires, they had locked hands and prayed: "Lord, use this machine to your glory."

Now Travis looked at the damaged plane, covered in dirt and cornstalks. He could not understand why this accident had happened. But he knew one thing: *Chief Tariri* needed to be repaired.

That night as the JAARS crew gathered in a hangar for a meal, Don Evans stood off to one side, alone and hurting. Travis went to him. Reaching into his pocket, he pulled out some money. "Here," he said, giving it to Don. "Maybe this will help if the insurance doesn't reach."

Don's eyes filled as he looked at the money. One crumpled dollar, a quarter, three dimes and a nickel. "Thanks, buddy," he choked out. The emotional burden Don was carrying began to slide away. It was a turning point for Don and he somehow knew *Chief Tariri* would be okay.

A hangar was made available for repairs on *Chief Tariri*. The plane was damaged but it was repairable.

Once again, God's faithfulness was obvious.

After the crash in Ohio, Bob Griffin wrote in a JAARS publication: "There is a real spiritual battle going on in the heavens over this plane for Africa...(but) God doesn't do anything by accident. Our responsibility is to trust Him...."

The DC-3 crew and the whole extended family of JAARS had seen God's faithfulness countless times. They knew they could trust Him.

And on June 27, 1992, *Chief Tariri* lifted into the blue skies over North Carolina and began its 6,994-mile trip to eastern Africa.

WINGING SERVICE TO AFRICA

On July 4, 1992, a tiny speck in the sky over Nairobi, Kenya quickly roared into the shape of a DC-3. Not any ol' DC-3, mind you—but *Chief Tariri*. Years of prayers and work culminated in that touch down. At long last *Chief Tariri* had arrived for service in eastern Africa, in a cooperative effort of JAARS and African Inland Mission's AIM-AIR.

Soon *Chief Tariri* had a busy schedule flying Bible translators and other missionaries to Zaire. The crew had the satisfaction of taking newly arrived families and their goods, within days of their arrival, to their assignments. In the past their goods came bit by bit over a period of weeks on smaller planes. *Chief Tariri* can carry five and a half times the load of the Cessna 206, the most commonly used plane in mission aviation.

Chief Tariri has a lot of "firsts" in its log book. The plane had not been in Africa long when it added another. It was scheduled to carry missionaries to their annual conference. The morning of departure, word came that bubonic plague had broken out at the conference site. Hurriedly, other arrangements were made and *Chief Tariri* ferried the group to their new conference site. Bubonic plague had to be added to the list of "firsts."

Chief Tariri soon logged another first in its history when a pilot took his daughter and family to their translation assignment. Jim Rainsberger recalls with teary eyes: "Carole and I brought each of our girls home from the hospital and dedicated them to the Lord. We've spent a lifetime praying for them...for their walk with the Lord, their future mates and so forth. Carole and I couldn't be translators—that's not our gift. But we ended up raising one! What a thrill to take Cindi and Jon (Hampshire) and their two little girls over

to Zaire in the DC-3 and help them set up for their translation project!"

The faithful DC-3 also started doing one of the things it does best: carrying large loads of cargo. It began to make famine relief flights to several locations in Africa. Somalia was first. "Flying into Somalia, where you know people have been shot to death over the relief food, really makes you stop and think. And you get people praying," says pilot Don Evans. "But Somalians were starving. You just have to do what you think God is asking you to do."

Rwandan refugees were added to *Chief Tariri's* log of service when the plane carried relief personnel and goods for Samaritan's Purse. Franklin Graham, International Director of the relief organization, commented on how exciting it was to see the Lord make possible a way for His people to "plant the Cross of Christ in an area of tragic suffering and need."

The flights to aid Rwandan refugees were made possible partly through the intervention of His Excellency, Daniel arap Moi, President of the Republic of Kenya. President Moi has a lifetime special fondness for Africa Inland Mission, as he was a student in their schools. After the relief flights, the President warmly received Mr. Graham and AIM personnel who extended their thanks for his cooperation and assistance.

The flights also were made possible by crew members following the Lord's leading. *Chief Tariri* pilot Scott Paulson remembers returning to the hangar after being out on a flight from 6:00 a.m. Tuesday through 3:00 p.m. Saturday. They learned a fellow pilot had radioed in, insisting on scheduling the DC-3 on Sunday. Normally mission planes do not fly on Sundays.

The crew quickly started loading tons of cargo, fueling and so forth. Paulson says: "That flight took extra faith...for us to believe that this was an important request and needed to be heeded without knowing what the outcome would be."

What was so urgent? Samaritan's Purse had been given the opportunity to work in a refugee camp only if they were at the Uganda/Rwanda border with the goods and personnel at 7:00 a.m. Monday morning.

"Up until that point," Paulson recalls, "Christian organizations had been severely hindered in their attempts to help with the refugees. If they did get permission to work in some camps, they were not allowed to have any religious work as well. Now Samaritan's Purse had a chance to be in charge of a whole refugee camp!

"So, Sunday morning," continues Paulson, "we were in the air flying to deliver the goods. We made the delivery on time, and headed home. Often, we as pilots only see or hear part of the story. But in this case we've heard a lot of encouraging things. Apparently, there were several agencies at the border waiting to cross, but the leader of that refugee camp came and got the Samaritan's Purse team and their goods and took them in. Since then the Lord has allowed them to be shining witnesses for Him!"

Franklin Graham says: "Time magazine quoted a missionary as saying 'There are no devils left in hell—they are all in Rwanda.' I can understand how someone could be moved to make such a statement after what I witnessed in Rwanda. But God has been working in that country. He allowed Samaritan's Purse to go into refugee camps when other agencies were being turned away. In addition to that work, we were asked to reopen the country's main hospital and have been allowed to establish a chaplaincy program there. We've also set up an orphanage. Many of those boys and girls saw their parents' brutal murders.

"When all is said and done," Graham continues, "the simple gospel message is what meets the needs of the human heart. Nowhere was that made more apparent to me than one afternoon when we were in Rwanda in our early days there. We noticed a little girl, seven or eight years old. She was hugging a blanket and rocking back and forth, softly singing.

"A soldier stood nearby with a machine gun draped over his shoulder. We asked him who this little girl was. He replied: 'She's an orphan just like all the others—an orphan.'

"'What is that she is singing?' we asked.

"'I don't know. It's something about God,' he

replied.

"We asked again, 'What are the words she is singing?' He listened for a minute and told us, 'She's saying something like "Jesus loves me, this I know." And she is saying it over and over.'

"We found out this little girl had watched as her entire family was murdered with machetes. The thing that sustained her was not the promise of a new government or a new house or even a better tomorrow—it was the good news of God's love, supremely demonstrated when His own Son was put to death on the cross for us."

Jim Streit, AIM-AIR manager, stated: "Without question, the DC-3 was intrinsic to the success of this operation. What an encouragement to see experienced, seasoned professional pilots who were willing to get right down and not just supervise but load and unload the cargo with everyone else....(the DC-3) has once again proven to be a reliable transport tool for mission groups...A large part of this must be credited to the DC-3 crew, who testify through their flexibility and servant hearts that they consider it a privilege to 'Serve Those Who Serve'."

Chief Tariri has carried relief goods within its host country, Kenya, too. Members of Bible Translation and Literacy, East Africa, a Kenyan organization, and members of its sister organization, Wycliffe Bible Translators, serve among the Rendille people in the northern desert. Suffering from prolonged drought, the Rendille were in need of powdered milk. BTL and WBT staff used their personal funds to purchase 50-kilo bags of milk and chartered the DC-3 to deliver them to the Rendille. "If that milk hadn't arrived when it did, we would have had 10 babies die within a day or two," Lynne Swanepoel, a Wycliffe Bible translator and literacy team member, said.

"We're happy to serve in any way we can," said *Chief Tariri* pilot Jim Rainsberger. "And we hope that as we try to meet people's physical needs, we're opening their hearts to discovering God's love through the Bible translation that's going on there."

Hearts also are opened to God's Word through

literacy all across Africa. The DC-3 has found itself in the school supplies business. The Ngbaka literacy program in the Democratic Republic of Congo grew directly out of the translation project. With 40,000 students, it is the largest literacy program in the Wycliffe world.

"We are in a rather remote location," says Wycliffe Bible translator Elaine Thomas with British understatement. "We're in the center of Africa. If you divided Africa top to bottom, and right to left, you'd find us close to the middle. And Africa is three times the size of the United States, so I'm told, or 50 times the size of Britain. The nearest telephone is in the next country. There is no mail service, so mail comes in from the next country by plane."

Elaine's colleague, Margaret Hill, adds: "Things have taken a turn for the better, with the arrival of the DC-3. This plane is a real help to us as it is opening up communications with the outside world.

"Before the plane was around," she continues, "if we wanted to get pencils for our 40,000 students, we had to send someone out to get 10 or perhaps five, or maybe 20 from little local market stores. No stationery shops. No way of ordering them from an office supply. One time the DC-3 came, we had 10,000 pencils and 10,000 pens come off the plane. This is a vast improvement!

"Then from the standpoint of our actually being able to travel," adds Margaret, "it's simply marvelous to get to Nairobi. We simply step on the plane here and 12 hours later, we step off in Nairobi. Before the arrival of the DC-3, if we were called to Nairobi for a seminar or workshop, or in our recent case, to check the final draft of the Bible, we had to go all the way to Cameroon, spend two days there and then travel to Nairobi. Very expensive. Very time consuming. So now we feel to some extent opened up to the outside world. It's helped communication, and it's helped our morale."

Bob Chipley, *Chief Tariri* mechanic and flight attendant, recalls with tears in his eyes, the flight to pick up Elaine and Margaret and the draft of the translated Bible. He says, "We picked up the ladies and

they had with them a box, about two feet by two feet by six inches. They had the draft of the complete Bible in the language they'd been working on for a long time. It was really neat picking them up and having just a small part in that work with those two ladies."

On another occasion, the DC-3 carried dignitaries and other guests to northern Kenya to witness God's Word return on camelback to the Rendille people. Return? On camelback?

Yes! A legend tells of God being close to the Rendille people generations ago. But one day a terrible thing happened. A stubborn woman insisted on moving her stick "igloo" house on the back of a camel instead of the usual goats. "Don't do it," people warned. "It isn't our tradition!" But the woman did not listen. As her camel walked across the desert, a stick from the house frame scratched the face of God. He became so angry He moved far from the Rendille people.

All these years, the Rendille people have believed in a supreme God, but they felt they could not communicate with Him. In August 1993 a crowd of people in the heart of Rendille-land jumped to their feet when two warriors leading camels appeared on the horizon. Tied to the camels' backs were cartons of the Gospel of Mark in the Rendille language. House frame sticks had been stuck in the packs, symbolic of God's interest in the Rendille people rather than His departure from them.

Brightly colored banners swung from the cartons declaring "The Gospel of Mark" in English and "The Good News That Mark Wrote" in Rendille. The Rendille word for "good news" sounds quite similar to the word for "water well." Thus, the Good News of Jesus Christ who brought Living, Eternal Water is tremendously significant to those living in both a physical and spiritual desert.

The red-robed warriors carried cartons of Gospels through the excited crowd. Elders, women and children, and other warriors pressed forward to watch. And among the group were Kenyan and foreign government officials, relief agency personnel, church leaders, missionaries and guests from as far away as North

America, Europe and South Africa. They had flown from Nairobi on *Chief Tariri.*

People seemed to hold their breath as the warriors cut open the cartons and held the Gospels aloft. Then cheers went up as one of the men, a recent literacy class graduate, read aloud from Mark.

The Reverend John Mpaayei, patron of the Kenyan Bible Translation and Literacy organization, told the group at the dedication: "God's Word is a light. When it comes to a place, it brings light and lights up other little lights."

Five hundred copies of the Gospel of Mark were printed. They sold out in minutes. One thousand more copies were ordered immediately.

Chief Tariri has been a faithful servant plane. And God has been faithful to it. The DC-3 has been called "the plane that changed the world." Certainly *Chief Tariri* has been a DC-3 that has continued changing the world, life by life!

ACKNOWLEDGEMENTS:

I am deeply thankful for the following people who helped with this book in a number of ways, including praying faithfully:

Lorrie Anderson
June Austing
Ruth Bishop
Bobbie Borman
Herb Brussow
Bob Chipley
W. R. Church
Rex Cogar
Vic Dickey
Paul Duffey
Don Evans
Wayne Fitch

Florence Gerdel
Virgil Gottfried
Franklin Graham
Bob Griffin
June Hathersmith
Elsie May Hartog
Don Hesse
Cal Hibbard
Don Johnson
Thelma Johnson
Pat Kelley
Sheri Borman Larsen

John Lindskoog
Mike McMillan
Shirley Minor
Kirby O'Brien
Jane Pappenhagen
Jim Rainsberger
Donna Simmons
Marianna Slocum
Elaine Townsend
Carolyn Young
Ethel Wallis
Ida Wells

Special acknowledgement of Willis Baughman who granted an interview just before he "flew" heavenward to be with his Lord. Also to Roy Minor who told me about some of his experiences with the plane and the people he flew. Roy appreciated those experiences so much he mentioned them in his last letter to friends and family before he went to Glory, too. And Jamie Buckingham, who left this earth, before I really got started on the manuscript. His book *Into the Glory* was a help and inspiration. Also I appreciated George Tilt, who remembered a lot for me. Now he's with his buddies in Heaven.

A further note: Chief Tariri died in his Peruvian jungle home in 1994 at the age of 80. Although he suffered from congestive heart failure, he continued to tell people about the Lord. Chief Tariri's last days were spent in his hammock, making up songs about his Savior.

—Karen Jane Lewis